Blessings of Age

A Pastoral Message on

Growing Older

Within the Faith Community

A Statement of the U.S. Catholic Bishops

UNITED STATES CATHOLIC CONFERENCE
WASHINGTON, D.C.

This statement was developed by the National Conference of Catholic Bishops' Committee on the Laity in collaboration with the Committee on Women in the Church and in Society. It was approved by the full body of bishops at their November 1999 General Meeting and has been authorized for publication by the undersigned.

> Msgr. Dennis M. Schnurr
> General Secretary
> NCCB/USCC

Photographs: Adobe Image Library (cover, title page); Rick Reinhard (pp. 2, 16); EyeWire (pp. 12, 20, 24)

Scripture texts used in this work are taken from the *New American Bible*, copyright © 1991, 1986, and 1970 by the Confraternity of Christian Doctrine, Washington, D.C. 20017 and are used by permission of copyright owner. All rights reserved.

First Printing, November 1999

ISBN 1-57455-341-0

Copyright © 1999, United States Catholic Conference, Inc., Washington, D.C. All rights reserved. No part of this work may be reproduced or transmitted in any form or by any means, electronic or mechanical, including photocopying, recording, or by any information storage and retrieval system, without permission in writing from the copyright holder.

Introduction

> There is an appointed time for everything, and a time for every affair under the heavens. (Eccl 3:1)
>
> Arriving at an older age is to be considered a privilege: not simply because not everyone has the good fortune to reach this stage in life, but also, and above all, because this period provides real possibilities for better evaluating the past, for knowing and living more deeply the Paschal Mystery, for becoming an example in the Church for the whole People of God.[1] (Pope John Paul II)

We are facing an unprecedented situation in the United States. At the beginning of the twentieth century, one in every twenty-five people in the United States was 65 or older. Today one in eight—a total of 33.2 million Americans—is at least 65. A person who reaches 65 can expect to live for seventeen more years; many live well beyond that.[2]

Both society and the Church are just beginning to grapple with the social, economic, and spiritual implications of this rapidly growing age group. The United Nations has designated 1999 as the International Year of Older Persons with the theme, "Towards a Society for All Ages." The Vatican, in its own contribution to the

International Year, has urged Catholics to make a new commitment not only to care for older persons but to learn from them.[3] Most recently, Pope John Paul II has offered his personal reflections on growing older.[4]

Inspired by this challenge, we, the U.S. Catholic bishops, offer this reflection on the experience of growing older within the faith community.

We speak out of profound gratitude for the many ways in which faithful and generous older Catholics have built—and continue to build—the Church.

We write as learners who together with older persons explore the period that some now call the "third age."[5] We learn from the many cultural heritages of our older people. Various customs, traditions, and contributions tremendously enrich the Church.

We write as pastors who cherish the whole person, with his or her gifts and talents as well as limitations and vulnerabilities. We stand firm in opposing euthanasia, assisted suicide, and all that threatens the dignity and sacredness of human life.

In this pastoral mesage we address the entire faith community, but we speak a special word to (1) older people themselves, (2) caregivers, (3) the parish faith community—pastors, staff, volunteers, and all parishioners—and (4) younger adults.

> According to the Administration on Aging, "About half (52%) of persons 65+ lived in nine states in 1997. California had over 3.5 million, Florida 2.7 million and New York 2.4 million, Texas and Pennsylvania had almost 2 million, and Ohio, Illinois, Michigan, and New Jersey each had over 1 million."

OUR PURPOSES

- To affirm and challenge older people, acknowledging both the blessings and the losses of later life and recognizing that interdependence, not independence, is the true gospel value
- To form a fresh perspective, one that sees older persons as active participants in contributing to the Church's life and mission and in meeting the spiritual needs of its members
- To develop structures, especially in parishes, that encourage and facilitate the contributions of older people

We are all growing older, not just as individuals but as members of a faith community. The spiritual growth of the aging person is affected by the community and affects the community. Aging demands the attention of the entire Church. How the faith community relates to its older members—recognizing their presence, encouraging their contributions, responding to their needs, and providing appropriate opportunities for spiritual growth—is a sign of the community's spiritual health and maturity.

With length of days I will satisfy them. . . . (Ps 91:16)

Experts on aging often speak of three phases of later life, corresponding to ages (1) 65-74, (2) 75-84, and (3) 85 and older. By 2030, about seventy million Americans, or 20 percent of the population, will be over 65. The number of older persons in some ethnic populations will increase at an even faster rate. Many older people exclaim, "I never expected to live this long."

Our society is aging. Nevertheless, society still values youth over age, doing over being, individualism over the common good, and independence over interdependence. Stereotypes about aging persist, despite the growing numbers of healthy, active seniors in our parishes and communities. Significantly, three in four persons aged 65-74 and two in three of those 75 and over say their health is good to excellent. While individual seniors vary in their abilities, health, and emotional outlook, the perception of aging as a period of unrelenting decline and withdrawal from society is simply untrue.

The current situation is unprecedented. The sheer number of older people as well as their vitality, their longevity, and their own desire to give something back to society and the Church impel us to develop new pastoral responses. Former responses that saw older people solely as the recipients of care are not adequate.

We now address specific groups within the faith community.

To Older Persons

The just shall flourish like the palm tree,
shall grow like a cedar of Lebanon.
Planted in the house of the LORD,
they shall flourish in the courts of our God.
They shall bear fruit even in old age,
always vigorous and sturdy,
As they proclaim: "The LORD *is just;*
our rock, in whom there is no wrong." (Ps 92:13-16)

With affection and respect, we bishops—some of whom are also seniors—speak to you who have entered older adulthood. We invite you to reflect on who you are and how you relate to God and others at this stage of your life.

Called and Gifted for the Third Millennium, the U.S. bishops' 1995 pastoral statement on the laity, discussed the spiritual life in terms of four specific calls: to holiness, to community, to service, and to Christian maturity. Here we focus on how older persons may experience and respond to these calls, especially the call to holiness, which embraces all other calls and leads to wisdom.[6] This wisdom is a sign of Christian maturity. In doing this, we draw on our own pastoral experience as well as the reflections and insights that older persons like yourselves have shared with us.

THE CALL TO HOLINESS

While all are called to holiness, to "ever more intimate union with Christ,"[7] spiritual concerns often assume greater importance for older persons. Many of you now have the time and space to reflect more deeply and to act with greater moral grounding and vision. For more and more seniors, daily Mass is the heart of their spiritual life and the springboard for companionship with many peers. Some are called to a type of prayer known as contemplative prayer, in which words give way to a quiet, attentive listening to God. The diminishment of the senses that may happen in later life, often seen only as a negative, can sometimes foster contemplation. Many older persons experience a renewed enthusiasm for learning and seek out Bible study groups, small faith-sharing groups, and adult faith formation programs.

Aging can also entail a "crisis of meaning." In later life you begin to wonder if your life has made a difference to anyone—if it has meaning. You may engage in reminiscing or life review. You look back at the events and relationships in your life, recognizing what is good and constructive and letting go of mistakes and failures.

> *The National Council of Catholic Women has developed RESPITE (Renewal: Spiritual/Temporal) to support caregivers. The program provides trained volunteers to stay with older persons for a short period of time, thereby offering caregivers a much-needed break from their constant duties.*

While you cannot change past events, you can ask God to help you change your attitudes and perceptions of them. Some past failures might now be seen as events from which you learned. Perhaps dealing with difficult people has taught you about patience and respect for different points of view.

Reviewing the past can lead you to take action in the present. You may discover a need for reconciliation: to seek forgiveness or to extend it to others. The first person who may need forgiveness is yourself. You may also discover that God has a new task for you. A talent waiting to be developed or a skill too valuable to be retired can lead to wonderfully creative and fruitful activities.

Sadly, the biggest changes in later life often involve losses: of spouse or adult children; of friends, home, health, or career identity; and, finally, of one's very life. This stripping away of so much that is held so dear is a painful process, one that can seem almost unrelenting, especially in advanced years. It can, however, be a natural preparation for death—the ultimate stripping of externals—and eternal life in heaven.

"The parish nurse is the most promising development in parish-based support of the health ministry," according to the Catholic Health Association. More than 5,000 U.S. congregations of all denominations now have a parish nurse, who primarily trains and educates the community and conducts health screenings. Parish nurses can take on many of the health-related tasks that previously fell to pastors and parish staff, such as handling requests for assistance, recruiting and training volunteers to visit shut-ins, and helping older parishioners when they are discharged from hospitals.

Facing one's own mortality means recognizing that death is part of life. Every other phase of life—childhood, adolescence, and young and middle adulthood—has been lived in expectation of a next phase. The next phase after old age, however long and rich old age might be, is eternal life. Older persons develop a deeper appreciation that "for [the Lord's] faithful people life is changed, not ended."[8] Older adulthood is a time when one learns to accept the ultimate change in life called death. It is the doorway to full union with God and to reunion with loved ones. From that doorway, Christ calls you to join your suffering and death to his so that they become redemptive. They have a purpose. As St. Paul says, "In my flesh I am filling up what is lacking in the afflictions of Christ on behalf of his body, which is the Church" (Col 1:24).

While death is the ultimate loss, we also want to say a word about two particular losses in later life.

First, you probably worry about a decline and eventual loss of your own personal health. You fear becoming dependent on others, perhaps even becoming a burden. You may worry about being unable to communicate your desires regarding such serious matters as life support systems. Advance directives can help your loved ones know your wishes. You may worry about losing your home or not having the financial resources to sustain you through chronic illness or disability. For some, these feelings become so overwhelming that they ask others to help them end their lives.

These are serious concerns that you, your family members and friends, and your faith community must work together to address. Here, however, we must say this to you: There is nothing wrong with being dependent on others; interdependence, not independence, is the true gospel value. From birth to death, no one is ever truly independent. All of us need each other, more at some times than at others. Do not fear asking for and accepting help. Your dependency can be an occasion of grace both for yourself and for others.

Second, we address those who are widowed:

We mourn with you in the loss of your beloved spouse. Even in the midst of family and friends, you experience an emptiness that will never be completely filled. You may deal with confusing emotions including anger at your lost loved one, yourself, or God. We understand that the first year is especially difficult, as birthdays and anniversaries bring bittersweet memories. Gradually the good days will outnumber the bad, but this healing process takes time and patience. Although social interaction can be difficult, we urge you to stay in contact with your faith community. Many parishes offer bereavement groups and other support for those who are widowed.

Many of you tell us that working through your grief is the hardest thing that you have ever done. You speak of coming to the realization that since your own life goes on, God must have a plan and a purpose for you. You draw strength and direction from prayer, Scripture, and the sacraments. Many find renewed meaning in reaching out to others, especially those who have suffered similar losses. Perhaps these words from one of the Church Fathers will bring you comfort:

They whom we love and lose are no longer where they were before.
They are now wherever we are.
— St. John Chrysostom

GROWING IN WISDOM

Growing in holiness means dealing with life's inevitable losses. More positively, growth in holiness leads to wisdom. Although many cultures revere older people for their wisdom, wisdom does not come automatically with age. The experiences of a lifetime have sown the seeds, but they must be cultivated by prayer and reflection on those experiences in light of the Gospel. With God's grace, as one matures, one arrives at wisdom: the realization that we come from God and are going to God. Or as St. Augustine said, "Our hearts were made for you, O Lord, and they are restless until they rest in you."

The wise person is always growing, always learning. The wise person is always connecting the past with the future. Elders share their stories, and in doing so, pass on what they have learned to future generations, through both words and example. Their wisdom does not die with them but guides and enriches generations to come.

THE CALL TO COMMUNITY

People become holy within a community. For most people, including older persons, the primary community is the family.

In his Letter to the Elderly *Pope John Paul II offers a moving personal reflection on the joys and sorrows of later life. Despite his own age-related limitations, the pope says, "I continue to enjoy life." He acknowledges his need for closer contact with other older persons and invites them to "reflect together on the things we have in common."*

You rejoice in additions to your family circle—daughters- and sons-in-law, grandchildren, great nieces and nephews. You pass on your family's cultural heritage through stories, celebrations and rituals. You worry about a child's divorce or a grandchild's exposure to drugs and violence. Some of you find yourselves in unexpected situations, such as caring for older family members or at the other end of the spectrum, for grandchildren. In the midst of change, you are often a point of stability, a steadfast example of faith deepened by the joys and heartaches of family life. For many, these are profound experiences of God's love and care.

Some of you experience the special joys of grandparenting. Freed from the responsibilities of day-to-day parenting, you give young family members the gift of unhurried time and attention. With the experience of years you can continue to encourage children to develop new skills or talents and to make important life decisions. As Pope John Paul II points out, you can "bridge generation gaps before they are made."[9]

Some of you are isolated from family members. You may be one of the last members of your family tree. Adult children may move away. You yourself may relocate. Spouses and siblings may pass away. After many years of normal family activity, you may feel alone, even abandoned by those you love most.

Many older people turn to parishes and parish-based small groups to find the community they need. As a family of families, the parish connects older adults with each other and with other generations. The parish provides spiritual and sacramental nourishment as well as social and service opportunities. Even here, however, some older people feel isolated or excluded. If you are confined to home or to an assisted living facility, parish visitation teams can keep you connected with the faith community. The staff and residents of such a facility might become another community for you.

> *Pope John Paul II's appeal to young people is well known, but in recent years he has also become a role model for older persons: "The Pope lives his old age with the greatest naturalism. Far from concealing it . . . he places it before everyone's eyes. With extreme simplicity, he says of himself, 'I'm an elderly priest.' He lives his old age in faith . . . He does not let himself be conditioned by his age."*
>
> —The Dignity of Older People

Some of your peers may feel isolated because of a lack of transportation to parish activities. Perhaps someone you know simply needs a personal invitation, a reassurance that he or she is wanted and welcomed. Especially during transition times people need the support of a caring community, but they can hesitate to reach out for it.

If you have received the gift of such a community, we ask you to share it with other older adults. For example, invite them to attend Sunday Mass and if possible, offer them a ride. Offer to introduce them at the next meeting of the parish seniors group. Invite them to help make sandwiches for the local soup kitchen. Reach out to another person, and draw him or her into a caring community.

Finally, the faith community can be the fertile soil in which life-giving friendships blossom. Here you often find men and women who share your values and experiences—people who understand the particular losses and fears of later life but whose faith gives them strength and courage. These friendships, often unexpected, can lighten the cares and multiply the joys of later life.

THE CALL TO SERVICE

The children have left home, and your retirement celebration has been held. Since most workers retire before age 65, a retiree can expect to have fifteen or more years for volunteering and other activities.[10] What do you do now?

You can be tempted to turn inward, to focus solely on pursuing hobbies and leisure activities as the well-deserved fruits of your labor. But you also have the opportunity to give something back, to make a significant contribution to your Church and community and in doing so, to enrich your own life. We, the bishops, state this clearly: Older persons have a responsibility, commensurate with health, abilities, and other obligations, to undertake some form of service to others.

You have already rendered generous service to family members and others. Now you can continue and perhaps extend that service to help meet pressing needs in society and in the Church. Possibilities abound, from simple things like giving a neighbor a ride to the doctor, to more extensive volunteer opportunities in schools, museums, health care facilities, community shelters, and outreach programs such as Meals on Wheels. Your parish also needs and wants you: to serve on pastoral and finance councils, to lead

In 1997, 66 percent of noninstitutionalized older persons lived in a family setting. This percentage decreased in proportion with increased age, especially for women. Only forty-one percent of all older women lived alone, but more than half of those aged 85 and over lived alone.

—Administration on Aging

Nearly six percent of U.S. children, or 3.9 million, lived in a household headed by a grandparent in 1997, while no parent was present for 1.3 million children.

—U.S. Census 1997

Parishes can support and engage older persons in a variety of ways, such as these examples:
- *Examining ways to acknowledge age-related issues, such as caregiving, in the context of liturgy or other parish celebrations*
- *Involving seniors in the activities of the parish school and religious education program*
- *Creating volunteer opportunities within the parish and linking with the broader community*
- *Offering space for educational programs that help seniors and family members better understand the aging process and the benefits and services available to them*

Bible study groups, to teach the young, to visit parish members living in health care facilities, and to console the bereaved. You can also invite the younger members of your family and parish to consider a vocation to ministry as a priest or a religious or a lay minister. In some ethnic groups, older persons play an especially important role in encouraging younger people to enter church service. As Pope John Paul II says in his *Letter to the Elderly*, "The Church still needs you. . . . The service of the Gospel has nothing to do with age" (nos. 13, 7).

Even if you are frail or homebound, your service to others can continue. You may now have the time to admire a child's drawings or praise a report card. You may be able to speak more honestly with family members or friends as they deal with sensitive issues. You may feel called to pray for the needs of your parish. You may want to pray about what you read in the newspaper or what you hear on the news. Ultimately, your example of steadfast faith in the midst of suffering can be a lasting gift to family and friends. What younger person, having witnessed the grace-filled final days of a parent or grandparent, cannot be attracted to that same faith?

We encourage you, and all of us, to find innovative ways in which to use the gifts and experience of older persons. As the Church and society grapple with difficult moral questions (such as end-of-life issues) and public policy concerns (such as health care and Social Security), the voices of Catholic seniors who have studied and reflected on these matters need to be heard. You are your own best advocates! Writing letters to the media and elected officials, speaking out at community forums, and developing grassroots organizations of seniors are some ways in which older persons can make a difference.

We also encourage increased opportunities for intergenerational activities. Mentoring a younger person is one example; so, too, are projects that draw on the combined skills of several generations. As bishops, we warn against a society and a Church that, however unintentionally, pits young against old. We do not believe that resources are so limited that the gains of one group come only through the losses of another group. Intergenerational activities can promote an appreciation of each generation's gifts and lessen misunderstanding and conflict between generations.

> *Caregivers who are Hispanic, African American, or Asian often have special needs. They are more likely to be caregivers; they are younger and more likely to have children under age 18; they have more health problems related to their caregiving tasks; and they are less likely to know of community services that could help them.*
>
> —Catholic Health Association of the U.S.

Caregivers

My son, take care of your father when he is old;
grieve him not as long as he lives. (Sir 3:12)

Increasing numbers of people are caring for relatives who need assistance. A 1996 survey found that one U.S. home in four had a person caring for an older adult. The lives of older persons and caregivers are intertwined: what helps one helps the other. We now speak to caregivers:

Some of you may have devoted your lives to this calling. We thank you for this service of love. As the number of frail older persons grows, we will look to you for guidance and offer our support in caring for them with respect and compassion.

Some of you never expected to find yourself in this role. You may feel unprepared. You may feel other emotions as well: love, concern, resentment, and frustration. This mix of emotions is normal, as you experience both the rewards and the stresses of caregiving.

Some of you are older persons yourselves, caring for another older person—most commonly, your spouse. Some of you are in especially difficult situations if your spouse faces terminal cancer,

Alzheimer's disease, or other serious illness. You face your own fears and uncertainties, yet the commitment you made to each other forty or more years ago remains unwavering and likely has deepened. In a skeptical world, where commitments are easily made and just as easily broken, you offer a much-needed and beautiful witness to fidelity. We thank you for this witness and pledge the Church's support as you continue to live out your commitment.

Some of you who are younger may be caring for parents or other older relatives. Caring for parents can be especially painful: you remember their earlier vitality, and you experience a sense of sadness and loss, especially as their physical and mental abilities decline. Eventually you may need to move your parent into a nursing home or assisted-living facility. This decision can be difficult and often produces feelings of guilt. In situations where a parent's health and safety, or perhaps your own health, require a change in living arrangements, we urge you to seek immediate assistance with these matters and to let go of this unwarranted guilt. Instead, focus on maintaining regular contact with your parents or older relatives through visits, phone calls, cards, and letters.

We also acknowledge those of you who serve the elderly in Catholic-sponsored long-term care nursing homes, assisted living facilities, as well as other types of residential, home, and community-based care. Yours is a holy calling. Some of you are volunteers in facilities that are under Catholic sponsorship and in others that are not, as lay ministers, eucharistic ministers, general pastoral care providers, and friendly visitors. You not only bring a blessing; you are a blessing.

The Catholic Church offers many skilled nursing facilities, assisted living facilities, and other daytime programs where dignified, compassionate care provides living witness to its mission. Through long-term care facilities, the Church cares for the most frail and vulnerable with specialized programs such as Alzheimer's care, pain management, and palliative care. The men and women who receive these services can also enjoy the consolation of their Catholic faith through Mass and sacramental celebrations. We know that caregivers themselves need care. The responsibilities of caregiving can be emotionally and physically exhausting. Some of you are simultaneously caring for children and older relatives. Many of you are employed; some of you have had to adjust work schedules. Finances can be a serious concern. Some of you who are priests and religious are also dealing with these issues. You have a right to expect support from:

1. *Other family members.* For practical reasons the responsibility for caregiving may fall primarily on one person, but other family members must assume their rightful share—for example, by contributing financially and arranging periodic respite for the caregiver. This is a matter of justice, not charity.

2. *Your faith community.* The parish has a responsibility to provide spiritual and other support for caregivers, for example, by helping to form support groups for caregivers, referring you to community resources, sponsoring adult education programs that deal with issues of particular concern to caregivers, or periodically recognizing and blessing caregivers.

Too often, however, as a Church and as a society we have not provided adequately for the needs of caregivers. As more people provide care—and as more people receive care for longer periods of time—we must respond to this new reality. We must look for ways to support caregivers who are themselves growing older, who are trying to balance multiple responsibilities, and who can expect to provide care for a number of years. Respite care is one possibility to explore.

To Pastors, Pastoral Staff, and Parishioners

The command to honor father and mother means that we should, individually and as a community, support, protect and respect older persons.[11] (Bishop Anthony Pilla)

We now address pastors, parish staff members and volunteers, and parishioners: Along with age come new experiences, new concerns, and new questions, all of which demand new approaches to pastoral care. As pastors, parish staff, and volunteers, you have the opportunity to anchor the aging experience firmly within a community of faith and to keep older persons connected to the community and the community connected with its older members. We hold up the vision of a vibrant, intergenerational community of faith where people of all ages and abilities both give and receive pastoral care.

Because parishes differ in their particular needs and resources, we offer a few foundational principles for parish ministry with older persons.

1. Older people are providers, not just recipients, of pastoral care.

Our first question should not be "How can the parish serve older people?" but instead "How can the parish receive and fully embrace the gifts of older persons?" Older people bring a wealth of spiritual resources, deep faith, skills, experience, and especially after retirement, time in which to offer them. Far from draining parish resources, older people are themselves a valuable resource. Even those who obviously need pastoral care—the homebound, the disabled, the seriously ill—are also able to give pastoral care, for example, by praying for their families, caregivers, and others, by sharing their own faith lives, or even through the simple yet powerful ministry of presence. By encouraging older persons to make their unique contribution, we affirm their dignity and value within the community of faith.

According to the Administration on Aging, "Minority populations are expected to represent 25% of the elderly population in 2030, up from 15% in 1997. Between 1997 and 2030, the white nonhispanic population 65+ is projected to increase by 79%, compared with . . . Hispanics (368%) and nonhispanic blacks (134%)."

2. Older people themselves should help to identify their pastoral needs and decide how they are met.

This is the principle of participation. Who knows better than older persons themselves what their needs are? Yet we marginalize older persons when we make decisions *for* them rather than *with* them. This can make them second-class citizens with the faith community and, equally sad, can deprive the community of their experience and wisdom.

3. Older people are as diverse, if not more so, than other generational groups.

They are women and men; they are single (never-married, widowed, separated, or divorced), married, religious, and clergy; they are from all races and ethnic backgrounds; they have a wide range of abilities and interests. They can differ in age from each other by twenty or more years. They defy stereotyping. They challenge the faith community to be as inclusive as possible in parish programming—for example, by remembering that older men, less numerous than older women, may need different types of service and social activities.

4. Older people need a mix of activities that connect them with each other as well as the larger faith community.

Older people, like most of us, need a group of peers with whom to share similar experiences, problems, and interests. Parish-sponsored seniors groups and daytime Bible study and service projects can bring together older persons for mutual support and friendship. We must take care, however, that seniors do not become isolated from the larger community. Parish service, social activities, and most important, Sunday liturgies will be richer when they attract a mix of generations. This means that

The Catholic Church has a long history of supporting older persons and their families. In 1997 Catholic Charities agencies provided social services to over 600,000 seniors and supported close to 700,000 seniors to meet emergency needs for food, shelter, and financial assistance. In the U.S., the Catholic community sponsors close to eight hundred long term and assisted-living facilities and many additional senior housing programs.

activities must be physically accessible to all, with transportation available if needed.

5. Spiritual health affects and is affected by the individual's physical, emotional, mental, and social health. While the faith community is especially concerned about meeting spiritual needs, it cannot ignore these other realities.

One parish cannot meet all these needs of the older person; however, the parish must recognize these needs and be able to direct older persons, their family members, and caregivers to appropriate resources. We encourage parishes to join with local providers of aging services that respond to the needs of older people. Moreover, within the larger community the Church should strive to be an advocate with and for older persons. In its preaching and practice, the Church can affirm the dignity and value of older persons in the human community.

We encourage pastors to study the impact of the increasing number of older persons on the parish. What do these demographic changes mean in terms of the parish's long-term vision, programming, budget, and staffing? We advocate a proactive stand that anticipates and meets older persons' needs as they arise and identifies ways of sharing the treasures of goodness, faith, and wisdom that older persons have to offer to enrich our faith communities.

To Younger Adults

*Insult no man when he is old,
for some of us, too, will grow old.* (Sir 8:6)

Each of us prepares for old age, and the way we experience it, in the course of our own life.[12]

Finally, we speak to younger adults:
Aging may be a topic far from your mind. You probably find it difficult to picture yourself as an older person. So did your parents and grandparents. Aging can bring up other realities—loneliness, frailty, dependency, suffering, and death—that few of us like to contemplate. We know that some of you have already encountered these realities in older friends and family members. We hope, however, that you also have positive images of aging: the eighty-year-old grandmother who delivers Meals on Wheels, the great-uncle whose routine includes daily Mass and a weekly golf game, or the elderly neighbor who sits on her porch and greets the children as they walk to and from school each day.

We know that at this stage in your life you are busy with

family, friends, job, and other activities. We ask you, however, as part of the faith community, to do the following:

1. Identify your own image of older persons.

If it is mostly negative, please look around you, especially in your own family and parish. Do you see older relatives who are still very much part of family life, whether attending a grandchild's game or recital, counseling an adult child, or hosting the family's Thanksgiving dinner? Do you see older parish members who proclaim the Word, teach the children, or present the annual financial report? Do you see homebound persons who make a daily offering of their prayers and limitations? We ask you to see these older persons as God's gift to you and to the entire faith community. Talk with them, learn from them, and draw inspiration from them. They can show you a whole new perspective on growing older.

2. Ask yourself, "What kind of person do I want to be in later life?"

The seeds for successful aging are sown in young and middle adulthood. Do you seek out and nurture friendships? Do you strive to deepen your relationship with God through prayer and sacraments? Do you give up some of your free time to serve others? These efforts, begun now, will bear fruit as you grow older. You will become that wise, loving person who has learned to enjoy all stages of life as the Creator's precious gift.

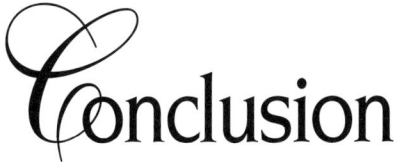

Conclusion

The only way to live well in old age is to live it in God.
(Linda Zaglio, age 101)[13]

In writing this reflection, we have spoken about a phenomenon that is, in many ways, entirely new. Our country and our world have never had so many older people—healthy, active, gifted older people. If we cannot foresee all the ways in which they will change society and the Church, we can say with certainty that change will happen.

We, the Catholic bishops of the United States, are pleased to celebrate this International Year of Older Persons by inviting older persons, their families, and their faith communities to help us develop new initiatives that encourage the participation of older persons in society and in the Church. We reiterate that aging is a gift to the entire faith community. When that community reflects the contributions of all—the old as well as the young—it will truly proclaim the ageless Christ present among us.

Questions for Reflection and Discussion

The following questions may be used for individual reflection or to promote discussion within parish pastoral councils, seniors groups, young adult groups, caregiver support groups, or in adult faith formation programs.

For Older Persons

- How do you continue to deepen your relationship with God in later life? What religious practices are especially meaningful to you? How have major losses—of family members, friends, health or mobility—affected your spiritual life?
- A younger family member asks, "Why do you spend time volunteering?" What do you answer?

For Caregivers

- In your own experience, what are the rewards and the challenges of caring for an older family member or friend?
- What kinds of support do you need as a caregiver?

For Pastors, Pastoral Staff, and Parishioners
- How does the parish use the gifts and experiences of older members? What else might be done to include them more fully in parish life? Are older people involved in parish decision-making, especially on issues that directly affect them?
- How does the parish bring together older and younger members and encourage them to learn from each other?

For Younger Adults
- Think about one or two older people whom you admire. What qualities in them do you especially admire, and how can you begin to cultivate those qualities now?
- What is your perception of aging? What are your fears? Have you talked with an older person to understand his or her perspective on aging?

The Catholic Health Association has provided a profile of caregiving for older persons:
- *"Caregiving usually involves women caring for women, often aged women caring for even more aged women."*
73 percent of caregivers are women.
- *In addition to their caregiving responsibilities, "almost two in three caregivers are employed at least part-time."*
- *The average duration of care is 4.5 years.*
- *"Care recipients are typically female relatives"; the average age of recipients is 77.*

—DATA COMPILED FROM A 1996 STUDY BY THE NATIONAL ALLIANCE FOR CAREGIVERS

A Pastoral Message on Growing Older Within the Faith Community

NOTES

1. Pope John Paul II, *The Vocation and Mission of the Lay Faithful in the Church and in the World* (*Christifideles Laici*), no. 48 (Washington, D.C.: United States Catholic Conference, 1988).
2. Bureau of the Census, "Sixty-Five Plus in the United States" (1995), <http://www.census.gov/socdemo/www/agebrief.html>.
3. Pontifical Council for the Laity, *The Dignity of Older People and Their Mission in the Church and in the World* (Washington, D.C.: United States Catholic Conference, 1999).
4. Pope John Paul II, *Letter to the Elderly* (Washington, D.C.: United States Catholic Conference, 1999).
5. Experts on aging sometimes use the term "third age" to denote that time in life when a person's primary work and/or the demands of parenting have ended. It follows the "first age," that of education, and the "second age," which is focused on production and one's life work. Since people move into the third age at different times, they choose when they want to define themselves as part of that age group.
6. National Conference of Catholic Bishops, *Called and Gifted for the Third Millennium* (Washington, D.C.: United States Catholic Conference, 1995).
7. *Catechism of the Catholic Church*, no. 2014 (Washington, D.C.: United States Catholic Conference, 1994).
8. *The Sacramentary*, Preface: Christian Death I, "The Hope of Rising in Christ."
9. Pope John Paul II, *On the Family* (*Familiaris Consortio*), no. 27 (Washington, D.C.: United States Catholic Conference, 1982).
10. Data from the U.S. Census Bureau and available from Internet releases.
11. Bishop Anthony Pilla, "The Needs and Talents of the Aged," *Origins*, November 8, 1984, pp. 328-334.
12. Pontifical Council for the Laity, p. 13.
13. Pontifical Council for the Laity, p. 12.

BIBLIOGRAPHY

Administration on Aging. "Profile of Older Americans: 1998" (<http://www.aoa.dhhs.gov/aoa/stats/profile/default.htm>, 1 February 1999).

Catholic Health Association of the United States. "Parish-Based Health Services for Aging Persons" (St. Louis, Mo.: Catholic Health Association, 1999).

U.S. Census Bureau. "Grandparents and Grandchildren." (<http://www.census.gov/population/www/socdemo/grandparents.html>, 10 November 1999)